Licensed to Hug

Licensed to Hug

How child protection policies are
poisoning the relationship between the
generations and damaging
the voluntary sector

Frank Furedi
Jennie Bristow

Civitas: Institute for the Study of Civil Society
London
Registered Charity No. 1085494

First Published June 2008
Second Edition October 2010
© Civitas 2010
55 Tufton Street
London SW1P 3QL

Civitas is a registered charity (no. 1085494)
and a company limited by guarantee, registered in
England and Wales (no. 04023541)

email: books@civitas.org.uk

ISBN 978-1-906837-16-7

Independence: Civitas: Institute for the Study of Civil
Society is a registered educational charity (No.
1085494) and a company limited by guarantee (No.
04023541). Civitas is financed from a variety of private
sources to avoid over-reliance on any single or small
group of donors.

All publications are independently refereed. All the
Institute's publications seek to further its objective of
promoting the advancement of learning. The views
expressed are those of the authors, not of the Institute.

Typeset by
Civitas

Printed in Great Britain by
Berforts Group Limited
Stevenage SG1 2BH

Contents

Authors

Frank Furedi is Professor of Sociology at the University of Kent in Canterbury. During the past decade his research has been concerned with the culture of fear in relation to issues such as health, children, education, food, terrorism and new technology. Since the publication of his study *Paranoid Parenting* (2001 & 2008), Furedi has explored problems associated with intergenerational relations, education and childhood. His recently-published *Wasted: Why Education is not Educating* (Continuum 2009) questions the way society educates children and young people and offers an alternative approach.

Jennie Bristow is a journalist and mother of two. She writes the 'Guide to Subversive Parenting' column for the online publication *spiked* (www.spiked-online.com) and is author of *Standing Up To Supernanny* (Imprint Academic 2009). Bristow edits the website Parents With Attitude (www.parentswithattitude.com) and is currently studying for a PhD.

Acknowledgements

We are grateful to the many individuals who helped us with their insights about the issues touched upon in this report. We conducted in-depth interviews with 18 individuals, who each gave up at least an hour of their time. We would like to thank them for their time and their thoughtful consideration of the issues we explore here. We also conducted an online survey using the web tool surveymonkey.com. We posted a link to the survey on a number of social networking websites, and collected 100 responses over the course of one month, the vast majority from individuals actively involved in voluntary activities with children. We would like to thank those who took the trouble to fill in this survey, adding their own thoughts and experiences, and confirming our hypothesis that vetting is an issue that is very much on people's minds.

Both editions of this publication have been made possible by a grant from the Nigel Lord Vinson Charitable Trust.

Foreword to Second Edition

Licensed to Hug was first published in June 2008 and sparked a public debate that highlighted the perverse effects of Government policy at the time. Under the guise of protecting children from abuse, heavy-handed regulations not only discouraged volunteering and undermined trust, but also created a false sense of security.

The Criminal Records Bureau can only have information about individuals who have already come into contact with the police. At any one time there will be people with paedophile tendencies whose inclinations are not yet known, with the result that there would be no official objection to them taking a job with children. To make matters worse, employers might even feel that they had fulfilled their obligations by paying for a CRB check and lower their guard.

No system of record-keeping can ever be an effective substitute for the kind of face-to-face appraisal that has been normal practice in organisations with a long record of successfully working with children. They have always used common-sense judgement to keep suspect individuals at bay. Ritual checking of criminal records has been a costly distraction.

In this revised edition the authors bring their argument up to date and respond to the announcement by Home Secretary, Theresa May, that the scheme is under review.

David G. Green

Introduction to the Second Edition

When *Licensed to Hug* was first published in June 2008, critics of the national vetting scheme were relatively few. While some serious civil liberties campaigners, media commentators and children's professionals had articulated grave concerns about the developing Vetting and Barring Scheme (VBS) and the legislation that underpins it,[1] there was no general outcry about a system that sought to prevent any adult from working or volunteering with children unless he or she had an official licence to do so, in the form of a check by the Criminal Records Bureau (CRB). The predominant response to the licensing of adults was a pragmatic acceptance that this was an attempt, however imperfect, to protect children from abuse, and as such it was better than nothing.

How that has changed. Now, the Vetting and Barring Scheme seems to be gaining the dubious distinction of being the most unpopular piece of regulation ever developed. It is rare to open a newspaper—any news-paper—without reading a story highlighting the absurdities and confusions caused by the scheme. From teachers and children's charities to celebrity authors and senior judges, prominent voices have raised practical and principled objections to the VBS and to the remit of the Independent Safeguarding Authority (ISA), the body charged with processing and retaining information about all those working and volunteering with children, including criminal convictions and 'soft intelligence' about allegations that may have been made against them.

In September 2009, Sir Roger Singleton, chair of the ISA, was forced to review the VBS, taking some of these concerns into account.[2] The Labour government later accepted all of these recommendations.[3] Speaking at a conference in September, Sir Roger said:

> We need to calm down and consider carefully and rationally what this scheme is and is not about. It is not about interfering with the sensible arrangements which parents make with each other to take their children to schools and clubs. It is not about subjecting a quarter of the population to intensive scrutiny of their personal lives. And it is not about creating mistrust between adults and children or discouraging volunteering.[4]

Two years ago, we argued that the national vetting scheme was indeed about all of these things—and unfortunately, we have been proven right. The VBS has interfered with parents' ability to make private arrangements, subjected a quarter of the population to intensive scrutiny of their personal lives, discouraged volunteering, and institutionalised mistrust between the generations. The architects of, and those charged with implementing, the VBS might take pains to stress its benign intentions, but in a short space of time the scheme's destructive consequences have acquired a momentum of their own.

The backlash against the VBS has raised serious questions about the legitimacy and workability of this system for licensing adults, and we hope that these issues continue to be interrogated in the public domain.

However, we also need to be realistic about the impact this debate has had on the ground. The principle that adults spending time with children who are not their own should have some kind of licence to do so has been widely accepted—and the confusion provoked by the backlash to the VBS has, if anything, encouraged organisations and individuals to be even more compliant with the scheme's demands.

Interfering with sensible arrangements between parents

In the preface, we observe that '[a]lready, the question "Have you been CRB-checked?" extends beyond the formal requirements of voluntary organisations to become part of everyday discussion at the school gates'. We argue that the VBS formally applies to adults working or volunteering with children, but that the logical consequence of demanding that some adults need to 'pass the paedophile test' is to set up an expectation that other adults, organising play dates or giving children lifts in their car, should have their motives similarly scrutinised.

In February 2010, the Department for Children, Schools and Families (DCSF) published a 'myth-buster' about circumstances in which the VBS will apply.[5] The key aim of this fact-sheet was to highlight that 'personal and family' arrangements were exempt from the VBS: that, for example, 'a parent who takes part in a rota with other parents to take each others' children to school once a week', or 'a parent arranging, with the parents of her child's friends, for the friends to stay at her home for a sleepover', does not need to be formally vetted.

This 'myth-busting' was issued in response to news headlines reporting that 'Parents who ferry children to clubs face criminal record checks': because, according to the requirements of the VBS, 'anyone working or volunteering on behalf of a third party organisation—for example, a sports club or a charity—who has frequent or intensive access to children or vulnerable adults will have to be registered with the scheme'.[6]

The distinction between parents volunteering on behalf of a children's club to ferry children around, and parents organising a rota between themselves for the school run, might be clear to policy-makers. But for people engaged in the real world of children's clubs, school runs, play dates and sleepovers, the line is far from clear: and the rationale for drawing it even less so. The messy, informal nature of working around children's activities means that it can be difficult to determine, exactly, when the impetus for organising lift-sharing comes from a club or from a group of parents; and in any case, why should somebody volunteering on behalf of the Scouts be more suspect than a father making his own arrangements to kick a ball around with a group of kids on a Saturday morning?

The attempt to draw such rigid distinctions between 'volunteering' and 'private arrangements' betrays officialdom's other-worldly understanding of community life. People are, understandably, highly confused by these rules, and it is an insult for Sir Roger Singleton to tell parents to 'calm down' about the confusion that his organisation has fomented. It is noteworthy that things have gone so far that a government should feel obliged to reassure parents that it does not intend to vet them before holding sleepovers for their child's friends.

In different times, we might expect that the absurdity of the rules around who should be vetted when would lead to a wholesale rejection of this regulation, with individuals prepared simply to ignore the compulsion to be vetted. However, as we note, the VBS has developed within a broader culture of suspicion surrounding relations between adults and children, which means that parents are predisposed to worry that other adults may pose a threat to their children. One uncomfortable outcome of the backlash against the VBS has been to highlight those excluded by the scheme—parents making sensible, personal arrangements with one another—and to raise the implicit question, 'Why should they not be vetted, when everybody else is?'

Vetting parents

Where the VBS has caused particular outcry has been in the suggestion that parents should be vetted for attending activities involving their own children. Headlines such as 'Now parents face criminal checks just to enter their children's school', 'Now even Sunday-school parents must be vetted', and 'Schools vet parents for Christmas festivities', have drawn attention to the expansionary quality of the vetting scheme.[7] We argue that the dynamic is towards issuing all adults with a 'probationary licence' before they can be trusted to interact with children. It was inconceivable that this dynamic would stop short of parents.

In February 2010, the Department for Children, Schools and Families took pains to state: 'It is not now, nor will it ever be, Government policy to vet parents just because they attend events that their own children are taking part in'.[8] Again, this assertion ignores the reality that adults interacting with their own children in public will generally be interacting with other people's children as well, and on that basis they can be targeted for vetting. For example, the above news story about parents being vetted to enter their own children's school relates to signs put up in Manor Community College in Cambridge, where pupils are aged 11-16, stating: 'We do not allow anybody who is not fully CRB checked to enter the college premises or to work unsupervised'. Defending the sign Ben Slade, the college Principal, said: 'We had a safeguarding review which suggested we should make it clear to people who are entering the building they are not to walk around unsupervised or work with children if they haven't been CRB checked... Ofsted [the schools inspection body] makes the rules up, not me, and a lot of schools have failed their inspections for not safeguarding pupils'.[9]

While we might object to Slade's zealousness, it is hard to fault his logic. Schools are, indeed, supposed to prevent non-vetted adults from spending time on their premises, and most of those adults are parents. How would the school distinguish the real parents from imposters? And what makes parents wandering around a school less suspect than plumbers or others who are subject to the vetting requirements?

A furious reaction greeted the story, in October 2009, that Watford Borough Council had banned parents from two of its playgrounds, stipulating that only council-vetted 'play rangers' would be allowed in while parents had to watch from outside a six-foot high perimeter fence.[10] The symbolism of this story is striking, in confirming our analysis of the way that the national vetting scheme seeks to create distance between the generations. Here, engaging in children's play is something to be done by officials, while other adults—including parents—stand uselessly by.

Again, Watford Council claimed that it was only obeying orders. A sign read: 'Due to Ofsted regulations we have a responsibility to ensure that every authorised adult who enters our site is properly vetted'. Council Mayor Dorothy Thornhill said: 'Sadly, in today's climate, you can't have adults walking around unchecked in a children's playground and the adventure playground is not a meeting place for adults'. Ofsted denied its responsibility for this initiative, with a spokeswoman claiming: 'Ofsted would never seek to prevent parents and carers having access to their own children'. But Ofsted, like the DCSF and the ISA, does not seem to recognise that drawing a rigid distinction between parents and their own children, and parents and other people's children, in real life is simply not possible. It is not surprising that organisations preoccupied with following official safeguarding procedures will err on the side of precaution, and rush in a blanket ban on all 'unchecked' adults.

The government has never demanded that parents be vetted in order to interact with their own children. But unless families are assumed to be living totally isolated lives, parents are likely to find themselves vetted anyway: because many volunteers for children's activities are also parents, or simply because they want to enter a public place such as a school or playground.

Scrutinising the personal lives of a quarter of the population

In the first edition of *Licensed to Hug*, we drew attention to the massive scope of the national vetting scheme: the number of adults who would be covered by the scheme, and the financial and time cost of this process. As the Independent Safeguarding Authority has come into being, these concerns have been borne out even beyond our fears. The escalating cost, scale and inconvenience of the VBS has been frequently challenged, with one newspaper warning of a 'children's care crisis' as vetting fees 'approach £600m'.[11] In July 2009, the *Independent* reported 'outcry' as it was revealed that 11 million adults would be included in the vetting database; following the government's review of the ISA, the media reported scant consolation as this estimated number dropped to nine million.[12]

It should be noted that even these large numbers are an underestimation. As we identified two years ago, one of the main criticisms that volunteers made of the national vetting scheme was the inconvenience of needing to obtain separate CRB checks for different organisations and get these updated. The ISA has attempted to streamline this process by bringing all the records into a centralised database, which can be accessed by relevant organisations and is updated with any new information. Once in operation, this will reduce the inconvenience of separate CRB checks — at a great cost to civil liberties, and massively expanding the scope of the vetting scheme. For once somebody is on the vetting database, he or she will stay there for life. The numbers can only grow, as new people are added.[13] Given the extent to which this scheme seems likely gradually to encompass all parents, as well as adults working or volunteering with children, the logic is that the *majority* of the adult population will sooner or later find itself on the vetting database.

The inclusion in the ISA's records of 'soft intelligence' about employees or volunteers has sparked considerable consternation. In October 2009, Britain's newly-established Supreme Court ruled that the system of investigating people's backgrounds for employment vetting is wrongly 'tilted' in favour of protecting the public, posing a threat to individuals' rights and representing a 'disproportionate interference' in people's lives.[14] Earlier in 2009, the outgoing Information Commissioner Richard Thomas warned that ISA's use of so-called 'soft intelligence', such as allegations or suspicions, combined with its power to ban an individual from a job, had the capacity to damage an innocent person in his or her career, 'financially and socially'.[15] Headlines such as 'Vetting blunders label 12,000 innocent people as paedophiles, violent thugs and thieves' and 'Innocent victims of CRB blunders receive just £223 compensation' indicate that the consequences of the inevitable errors that will be made by this vast technical system should not be regarded lightly.[16]

However, these well-founded civil liberties concerns have to contend with a powerful cultural acceptance of the idea that 'if you have nothing to hide, you have nothing to fear'. As we observe in *Licensed to Hug*, this sentiment formed the basis of many individuals' initial grudging acceptance of the VBS, and concerns about civil liberties tended to be outweighed by the idea that you cannot argue with a scheme that intends to protect children. As the civil liberties implications of the VBS have become more apparent, more people are openly voicing concerns. But even so, these are tempered by practicalities and pragmatics. If, as a parent wanting to help out on a school trip, you are told that you need a CRB check, it is hard to object without appearing as a suspicious character: and if you do object, you will simply be barred from the trip. So the predominant response by individuals is simply to comply with the rules, and hope that problems caused by false allegations or incorrect information will not happen to them: or not to volunteer in the first place.

Discouraging volunteering

In the first edition of *Licensed to Hug*, we noted how adults were already being deterred from volunteering by a generalised cultural suspicion of adults who want to spend time with children other than their own. We argued that mandatory CRB-checking would fuel this process by adding a further practical and emotional barrier to individuals' involvement. Rather than welcoming spontaneous offers of help, voluntary organisations have to demand that individuals complete paperwork and wait for the check to be processed; and rather than accepting individuals' goodwill, organisations have first to ask whether or not they are convicted paedophiles. Given that volunteers make no instrumental gain from helping with children's activities, we argued that the effect of putting such unpleasant barriers in the way would discourage people from offering in the first place.

As with the rules surrounding 'private arrangements', the officials are sensitive to the problem of creating barriers to volunteering, and to that end has revised and tried to clarify the rules about which volunteers need to be vetted, and when. This is a significant problem, as voluntary organisations are faced with legal or financial penalties if they do not comply with the requirements of the VBS. However, the requirements remain confusing and unclear. For example, organisations have to work through whether their volunteers have 'frequent' or 'intensive' contact with children. Initially, 'frequent' was defined as contact that takes place once a month, and 'intensive' was defined as contact taking place three times in every 30 days or overnight. Sir Roger Singleton revised the definitions, so that 'frequent contact' is now defined as contact that takes place once a week or more often with the same children, and 'intensive' as contact that takes place on four days in one month or more with the same children or overnight.[17]

It may be clear, from these new requirements, that a parent who goes into school once a week to help a class of children with their reading will need to be registered with the ISA, while a children's author going into a school on a one-off occasion will not. But the reality of voluntary work is that the nature and frequency of people's contact with children is not so easy to determine in advance. What about the mother who, at the last minute, volunteers to accompany a Scout group on an overnight camping trip, because another volunteer has fallen ill and without the requisite number of adults, the trip will not be able to take place? Or the father who steps up to the mark to be 'Santa' at his children's school?

Volunteering, by its nature, depends upon spontaneous and informal offers of help. But the Vetting and Barring Scheme formalises this process, by regulating all 'frequent' or 'intensive' volunteers as though they were professionals, or employees. In this respect, the more prepared an individual is to volunteer time and energy to help with children's activities, the more he or she is regarded as an object of suspicion and in need of a licence. Meanwhile, the letter of the law might not apply to more 'flaky' or occasional volunteers—the parent who helps out with the children's school disco, for example, or with a single fundraising day for the Brownies. But voluntary organisations, confused about the law and concerned not to be seen to be contravening it, are tending to adopt pre-emptive strategies that vet everybody, 'just in case' they fall foul of the law.

Often the argument put forward is that many people who volunteer for occasional children's activities have already been vetted, because they work with children or they are otherwise involved in more formal voluntary work. The pragmatic argument that others 'might as well' be vetted too speaks to an implicit acceptance that there are two tiers of adults in society: those who are ISA-registered, and those who are not. This has fuelled a further disturbing trend, whereby the existence of formal vetting procedures can feed and seem to justify the officiousness that some members of voluntary organisations have always exhibited. For example, a father who is heavily involved in his sons' youth football club told us that some other parent volunteers seem to have adopted a policing role, constantly checking whether other parents have been vetted or are following accepted procedures laid down by the club's child protection policy.

Creating mistrust between adults and children

It is important to recognise that the willingness of organisations and individuals to go along with the strategy of mass vetting, often going further than they are legally obliged to, cannot be accounted for merely by the existence of a confusing law. The idea that volunteers 'might as well' have a CRB check 'just in case'; that those with 'nothing to hide' have 'nothing to fear'; that registering with the ISA is merely a pragmatic action, and something that those who want to volunteer for children's activities 'just do'—these sentiments speak to the way that being vetted is rapidly coming to be seen as a mark of responsible adulthood and, indeed, parenthood. If a responsible parent is one who becomes engaged in voluntary activities involving other people's children, then a responsible parent will be vetted and cleared by the Independent Safeguarding Authority.

In this respect, the establishment of the Vetting and Barring Scheme has intersected with a broader culture of fear, to create a formal barrier between adults and children. The reformulation of the idea of 'responsibility' in terms of somebody who has been officially licensed has significant implications for the future of inter-generational relations in our society. It has crystallised the assumption that adults who take responsibility for children should be somehow qualified to do so: that holding the status of an adult is not enough. Holding a valid CRB check, or having clearance from the ISA, has come to be seen in similar terms to having a First Aid certificate or teaching qualification—as though being officially cleared of child abuse gives these adults some particular knowledge of, and skill with, children, whilst the rest of the adult population is effectively blacklisted and cautioned to keep its distance.

Such formalisation of inter-generational contact will continue to make adults unsure of themselves and each other, and to create further tension between adults and children. We should also remember that, as one mother said to us, 'it won't make children safer'. By conceptualising child protection as a technical process of certification rather than a generational, human responsibility, the reverberations of the national vetting scheme leave children more at risk and ill at ease than ever before.

On 15 June 2010, the new coalition Government announced that registration with the Vetting and Barring Scheme would be halted and that a more proportionate and commonsensical scheme would take its place. Home Secretary Theresa May stated that the new scheme will 'take a measured approach' for dealing with the problem. This announcement, and the recognition by the Government that the existing system of vetting had got out of hand, is much welcomed.

However we believe that unless a radically new approach is adopted towards adult-children relations nothing much will change. It is essential that the Government upholds two fundamental principles for managing inter-generational relations. First, it is important to uphold and promote the idea that child protection is the responsibility of all adults living in a community and not a duty to be outsourced to specialists. Secondly, any scheme adopted has to accept the principle that adults are innocent until proven guilty and should not be subjected to a form of registration that assumes guilt until innocence is proved. What's required is not just a new system, but an enlightened approach towards the promotion of intergenerational contact.

Frank Furedi and Jennie Bristow
June 2010

Preface to the First Edition

From Girl Guiders to football coaches, from Christmas-time Santas to parents helping out in schools, volunteers—once regarded as pillars of the community —have been transformed in the regulatory and public imagination into potential child abusers, barred from any contact with children until the database gives them the green light. How has this development come about, and what is its effect on relationships of authority and trust in our communities?

When the first edition of my book *Paranoid Parenting* appeared back in 2001, some individuals in Britain and America had already mooted the idea that parents should be licensed, in order to weed out those who were abusive or otherwise unfit.[1] Their proposals attracted some discussion amongst academics, policy-makers and parenting professionals, and it was not uncommon for journalists to ask, often rhetorically: 'Isn't it strange that you need a licence to own a dog, while anybody can be a parent?' As I noted at the time, a trend was already underway to treat parenthood, not as a normal part of life, but as a professional endeavour that demanded increasing regulation and monitoring. The effect was not to create better parents; rather it was to decrease parents' confidence in themselves, and weaken ties of solidarity between parents and other adults, to the detriment of both family life and wider community relations.

Parents are not forced to carry licences (although with the launch of the National Academy for Parenting

Practitioners in November 2007, certificates in Adequate Parenting are surely on their way). But when it comes to other adults—non-parents, or parents of other people's children—a national licensing scheme is well underway. The horrific abduction and murder of two school-girls in the Cambridgeshire village of Soham in 2002 fuelled a chain of policy proposals that now mean that anyone who works with children in any capacity, along with volunteers who help out at children's clubs, are required by law to have undergone a centrally-administered vetting process through the Criminal Records Bureau (CRB).

While you do not yet need a licence to parent your own children, you certainly need a licence to interact with anybody else's. Already, the question 'have you been CRB-checked?' extends beyond the formal requirements of voluntary organisations to become part of everyday discussion at the school gates. One mother of an eight-year-old recounts:

> My daughter is allowed to play out in the street with kids from the neighbourhood. She said she was going to Semih's house and I said OK. Ten minutes later Semih's mom knocked at my door and said, 'I must introduce myself as we haven't met.' I thought she was going to tell me her name, have a chat, but she said she was CRB checked and her husband was CRB checked and then went away. I still don't know her name!

When parents feel in need of official reassurance that other parents have passed the paedophile test before they even start on the pleasantries, this indicates that something has gone badly wrong in our communities. Over the course of their young lives, children will interact with a number of adults outside their immediate families—teachers, sports coaches, Scoutmasters, bus-drivers, passers-by who stop to give them directions or help them out when they are in trouble. As a society, we appreciate that children need these other adults to broaden their horizons, educate and challenge them, contain their behaviour, provide support and generally take responsibility. Throughout our history informal and unregulated collaboration between grown-ups has provided the foundation for the socialisation of young people. This form of collaboration, which has traditionally underpinned intergenerational relations, is now threatened by a regime that insists that adult/children encounters must be mediated through a security check.

Before they can be counted on to play a positive role in children's lives, adults today have to be in possession of a piece of paper showing that they are not likely to be a malign and dangerous influence. In other words, they cannot be trusted to be in the proximity of a child unless they possess a *probationary licence* to be responsible adults. Implicitly the licensing of adulthood undermines its authority. It encourages the disassociation of adulthood from trust and respect. Adulthood no longer possesses authority over children—it requires the legitimation of a security check before its authority can be exercised. The institutionalisation of the vetting of grown-ups also communicates powerful signals about the role of adults. Adults are no longer trusted or expected to engage with children on their own initiative.

Vetting encourages the cultural distancing of generations. As a result, intergenerational encounters have lost some of their informal and taken-for-granted dimensions, and many such encounters are rendered troublesome and awkward.

The cultural distancing of generations weakens the bonds of community life. Today, despite an official recognition that communities are increasingly atomised and individuated, government policy implicitly fuels this process of fragmentation through policies that encourage the erosion of the collaboration of the older generations in the joint enterprise of socialising youngsters. Specifically policies encourage parents to shy away from their instincts to trust each other and to put their faith only in those who can show their probationary licence on demand. The speed at which the acceptance of CRB checking in formal settings has filtered through to the wider community of parents, who wonder 'how they can know' it is safe to let their child go home with the parent of a friend, illustrates the unforeseen and often destructive consequences of using interpersonal regulation as a Band Aid for a more complex cultural problem.

The evidence of history indicates that one of the ways that communities are forged has been through the joint commitment of adults to the socialisation of children. That is why in most communities all grown-ups—and not just parents or those who have children —are expected to introduce children into the norms of the community, protect them against hazards and if necessary reprimand anti-social behaviour. But what happens when the exercise of such responsibilities become subject to formal vetting and regulatory procedures? The aim of this report is to explore this development and in particular to examine its impact upon adults engaging voluntarily with children's activities.

In raising certain problems caused by the growing formalisation of relationships that were previously marked by the qualities of being informal, spontaneous and taken for granted, we do not assume that the cause of these problems is one particular legislative development such as CRB checking, or that the solution is as simple as merely overturning the legislation. In our view, the assimilation of vetting above all provides a potent symbol of the contemporary problem of adults, children, risk and trust, and the way that regulatory attempts to resolve this problem have an unfortunate tendency to exacerbate it. In the current climate, the routine police vetting of adults:

- Fuels suspicions among adults about each other;

- Transmits negative signals about adults to children;

- Undermines the ability of adults to take responsibility for children;

- Diminishes adult authority and damages community relations.

We believe that ultimately parents want, and need, to be able to make a few very clear and simple assumptions about adults in general:

- They can play an important part in enriching children's lives;
- They will step in to help children who are in trouble;
- They can be relied upon as a source of solidarity and support.

Our research indicates that positively, many adults in today's society continue to be willing and able to play this role. The problem is that it is not taken for granted that they will do so. None of the desired objectives raised by individuals in relation to children's safety can be realised when the routine police vetting of adults becomes the norm.

Frank Furedi
April 2008

Summary

1   One of the most disturbing symptoms of inter-generational problems is the erosion of adult authority.

2   A one-dimensional focus on the risk management of childhood has led to the formal monitoring and policing of intergenerational encounters.

3   The police vetting of adults has contributed to the fuelling of mistrust towards the way that grown-ups behave with children.

4   Attitudes of suspicion reinforced by official vetting have discouraged adults from spontaneously engaging with children.

5   Intergenerational relations are increasingly reg-ulated through rules and have become increasingly formal.

6   The vetting of adults is not an effective instrument for protecting children and in practice works as a form of impression management. It provides a rit-ual of security rather than effective protection.

7   One of the unintended hazards of vetting is that it encourages a flight from professional judgement about how best to respond to children's needs. People who expect the system to bring problems to light are often made to feel redundant in the management of intergenerational relations.

8 The formalisation of intergenerational contact contributes to the deskilling of adulthood. If adults are not expected to respond to problems in accordance with their experience and intuition they will have little incentive to develop the kind of skills required to manage children and young people.

9 The cumulative outcome of the trends discussed is to discourage adults from taking responsibility for the welfare of young people. These trends have fostered a climate where *responsibility aversion* becomes the defining cultural norm through which many adults respond to the world of children.

10 On the basis of analysing the available evidence we have drawn the conclusion that confronting the culture of responsibility aversion is a precondition for reconnecting adult authority with the world of children.

1

CRB Checks:
Barriers to Involvement

In November 2006, the Safeguarding Vulnerable Groups Act was passed into law. One of the key components of this legislation was the creation of an Independent Safeguarding Authority (referred to in the legislation as an Independent Barring Board), a 'new Non-Departmental Public Body' designed 'to take consistent expert decisions as to who should be barred from working with children and/or vulnerable adults'. The Independent Safeguarding Authority (ISA) 'will be the most stringent vetting and barring service yet', claims a government consultation document published in November 2007.[1]

The ISA is but the latest in a string of government initiatives to ensure that only people who are properly vetted have contact with children other than their own. Stating that: 'Nothing can be more important than ensuring that children and vulnerable adults are properly safeguarded', the 2007 consultation document lists ten measures that the government has taken since 1997 in order to strengthen such safeguards: on average, one measure per year. One of those measures was the establishment of the Criminal Records Bureau (CRB) in 2002, initially designed to streamline the existing vetting process undergone by teachers and other key professionals working with children.

Since 2002, a steadily-expanding category and number of people have found themselves required to undergo a CRB check simply because their work or voluntary activities may bring them into contact with children. This includes football coaches, cricket umpires, Guiders and Scoutmasters, volunteers in churches, charities and community centres, parents who volunteer for school trips or after-school clubs, and members of parent-teacher associations—as well as a host of people whose work is not to do with children but might involve them having some potential contact with them, such as bus drivers, or plumbers who fix school radiators.[2]

The expansion of vetting has been phenomenal. In autumn 2006, prior to the passage of the Safeguarding Vulnerable Groups Act, the London-based Manifesto Club launched a campaign warning against the 'damaging' impact of ever-more stringent vetting procedures on adult/child relations. It noted that there had been a rise of almost 100 per cent in the annual number of criminal checks issued by the Criminal Records Bureau (CRB) since 2002, leading to ten million disclosures having been issued by 2006. In a letter to *The Times* a number of high-profile critics of the Safeguarding Vulnerable Groups Bill observed:

> The Bill will mean that up to a third of the adult working population—those who come into contact with children through their work or volunteering—will be subject to continuous criminal-records vetting.[3]

In April 2008, responding to ↳
timetable for the implementation of the
Vulnerable Groups Act, the Manifesto Cₗ
that the new Act will affect 'two million more
than expected', with the government now estimₑ
that 11.3 million adults will have to comply with thₗ
law; and that the new vetting and barring scheme
would cost £84 million to set up, more than five times
the original estimate. 'The escalating costs, scope and
size of the government's vetting scheme are a sign that
the scheme has no clear rationale', argues the
Manifesto Club's briefing document. 'Costs and
coverage could well inflate still further. The Act's
boundaries are irrational and confusing, and are likely
to prove difficult to communicate and enforce.'[4]

Since 2002, an ever-expanding proportion of the UK
adult population has had to be granted a probationary
licence to behave like an adult: to work with, interact
with, and take responsibility for, children. For those
committed to stringent vetting systems, this may seem
like a good result. It implies both that a large section of
adult society can, after all, be trusted with children,
and that the system is working to keep out those who
cannot. The idea that the only people who should be
worried about CRB checks are those with 'something
to hide' is widespread. In this sense, the fact that
vetting creates barriers to involvement in voluntary
work is seen as a positive development, as it serves to
keep out only those who should not be there in the first
place.

However, our experience of vetting as a society raises a question mark over the idea that the system 'works': either in terms of protecting children from abuse, or in terms of increasing public confidence in those working or volunteering with children. As the recent history of the Criminal Records Bureau has shown, the first consequence of more stringent vetting procedures has been the demand for even more stringent security procedures. This indicates that the effect of CRB checks is less to increase trust in those organisations and institutions that insist upon vetting than it is to fuel mistrust in those that do not.

Experience indicates that the institutionalisation of the vetting of adults has unleashed an expansive logic towards increasing the number of people who are deemed to be in need of formal clearance. So in February 2008, the government announced trials of a new scheme that will enable parents to check with police whether a 'named individual'—a family member, a neighbour who looks after children, a new sexual partner—has child sex convictions.[5] Home Secretary Jacqui Smith stressed the initiative would not be a 'community-wide disclosure', with information given out to anyone who asks. But the more this process goes on, the more arbitrary it becomes to say where vetting should stop, and trust begin.

Has the impact of vetting upon child protection been positive or benign? It is difficult to answer this question without taking note of the practical barriers caused to adults' voluntary involvement with children by mandatory vetting procedures. At the very least they have added to the cultural unease about what role adults can, or should, play in relation to other people's children; contributing to the consolidation of a situation where intergenerational interaction is increasingly guarded and fraught with tension.

History of the CRB: vetting begets vetting

The work of the Criminal Records Bureau (CRB) was thrust into the limelight in September 2002, in a political debacle that rocked the then Education Secretary Estelle Morris. When it had become apparent, several months earlier, that the CRB could not cope with the sheer amount of work involved in vetting teachers before the start of the new school term, the Department for Education and Skills (DfES) had pragmatically instructed schools to accept the previous check, based on a check of police records and the List 99 'blacklist', for teachers awaiting CRB clearance. But in August 2002, two Cambridgeshire schoolgirls, 10-year-olds Jessica Chapman and Holly Wells, were murdered, and school caretaker Ian Huntley (along with his girlfriend, teaching assistant Maxine Carr) were arrested.

With the start of school term looming, the government immediately called a halt to interim arrangements and demanded that all new staff must obtain full clearance before starting work. Chaos ensued, with 8,600 background checks on teachers still outstanding at the beginning of the new term and some schools staying closed for extra days while others barred non-vetted teachers from the classrooms.[6] The DfES had to recant this decision at the start of term, faced with the realisation that it had no idea how long it would take for the vetting to be completed.[7]

In 2006 Ruth Kelly, who was Education Secretary by this time, faced a similar crisis when caught between the problems caused by the national shortage of teachers, and the ever-more stringent checks on those willing to apply for the job. To outcry from the press, the DfES had decided that, as all sexual offences are not of equal magnitude, a selection of individuals on the Sex Offenders Register should not automatically be included on the List 99 'blacklist' that would prevent them from working with children ever again. Caught on the defensive, Kelly tried to reaffirm her commitment to vetting by opening another can of worms, and commissioning the schools inspection body Ofsted to investigate school records of staff vetting. Ofsted found major flaws in the way many schools kept such records, which led to thousands of teachers having to be re-checked at a cost of tens of thousands of pounds, and yet another blow to public confidence in the ability of vetting systems to weed out convicted sex offenders.[8]

These high-profile CRB scandals have all focused on schools—where vetting for several years has been accepted as necessary, and where teachers are paid professionals, looking after children day in, day out. Even here, it is possible to identify a pattern whereby the aim of stringent vetting systems—to prevent any individual from ever harming a child in his or her care—will never be met. Aside from the fallibility of record-keeping and technical systems, vetting only takes into account what somebody has done in the past. The most sophisticated system in the world cannot anticipate how individuals with a clean record might behave in the future. Thus the CRB provides little guidance about people's behaviour in the future. It provides the impression of security but not the substance.

This goes to the heart of the problem with the Criminal Records Bureau. Since its inception, the work of the CRB has been relentlessly politicised by government—to the point where vetting schemes are justified in terms that make no real sense. The clearest example of this relates to Ian Huntley, the school caretaker who murdered the two Soham schoolgirls. As has been widely remarked, it is highly unlikely that a CRB check would have stopped Huntley from coming into contact with his victims: he did not work at their school, and though he had been suspected of sex offences in the past, he had never been convicted. Yet Estelle Morris' panicked reaction to the Soham murders put CRB checks on the agenda, and the government subsequently commissioned an inquiry into the murders, chaired by Sir Michael Bichard. The 2006 Safeguarding Vulnerable Groups Act—which creates 'the most stringent vetting and barring service yet'—was introduced 'specifically' in response to recommendation 19 of the Bichard report, which 'proposed requiring the registration of those who wish to work with children or vulnerable adults'.[9]

The Soham murders continue to provide the justification for new vetting initiatives. The ministerial foreword to the 2007 DCSF/Home Office/DH consultation document on the Independent Safeguarding Authority thus begins:

> The tragic murders of Holly Wells and Jessica Chapman in Soham in 2002 highlighted clearly and painfully the areas for improvement needed in the safeguarding systems at the time.[10]

One problem with politicising child protection measures in this way is that it leads to unrealistic expectations about what such measures can achieve. As Eileen Munro, reader in social policy at the London School of Economics and an expert in child protection systems, argues: 'The Bichard report in no way shows how [vetting] could have prevented the deaths of those two girls.' It should be possible, says Munro, to make a simple screening check to ensure that people working with children are not serial paedophiles, but the current national vetting scheme is a 'fantasy precaution', based on something entirely different to addressing a practical concern. It represents the dangerous combination of 'a risk-averse society plus the fantasy that we can avoid risk completely'.[11]

It is difficult to avoid the conclusion that the national vetting scheme represents an exercise in impression management rather than offering effective protection. Some forms of impression management are just a harmless public relations exercise. For example unnecessary warnings about every possible side effect on patient leaflets accompanying medicines do not protect anyone but neither do they harm them.

However vetting measures not only offer fantasy security; they also fuel suspicion about adults. In that sense they are not just a harmless ritual but a negative influence over the conduct of adult/children relationships.

Views about vetting

In our research for this report, we designed a small online survey that we posted around a number of social networking sites used by parents and volunteers. The respondents to our survey, most of whom were actively involved in volunteering (and had been CRB-checked themselves), thought that a system of national vetting was necessary. For some, it seemed like common sense:

> *To protect those who can be trusted, for those parents who are less trusting and more suspicious of adults wanting to work with children, means that those who are involved have been checked and are 'ok'.*
>
> *Female Guider, aged 25-30, South East.*

> *I do think it's absolutely necessary. If we are to trust our children in other people's care we need to know they will be entirely safe.*
>
> *Female, aged 18-24, North East. Not engaged in voluntary work.*

A handful seemed more sceptical:

> *Suppose it is necessary to find the tiny 0.00001 per cent of people who might be dangerous to children.*
>
> *Female Guider, 31-40, London.*

Now it's started—it can't be done away with. It's made many people think about the issues and actually caused concerns and paranoia that shouldn't have been there.

> Female, aged 31-40, South East. Runs a church children's holiday club and teaches French at school on voluntary basis.

Many, however, prefaced their statement that CRB checks were necessary with the word 'Unfortunately'. The sentiment behind this was summed up by a Scottish woman, aged 31-40, who hoped to become involved in volunteering when her children were older:

It is sad but in this day and age it is necessary.

Vetting is not viewed as a positive development so much as a necessary evil, arising from a society that is at greater risk of child abuse than before. However, as a precaution against child abuse, the flaws in the system are evident. When the respondents to our survey were asked how they thought the system could be improved, two major recommendations emerged. The first was a practical one, that the process is done more quickly and simply, and that checks are transferable between organisations:

A standard check for all activities involving children would make sense. Currently my wife has a CRB check to be a teaching assistant but needs another to be a football club volunteer. Presumably the same checks are made in each case, so why isn't the first check good enough? Also, the check takes far too long—one of the documentation items recognised is a household bill within the last three months. By the time they'd processed my application the three months had passed and they required another.

> Male under-8s football coach, aged 31-40, Norfolk.

Simplify the paperwork, speed it up and make CRBs transferable. I have 5, that's TOTALLY unnecessary. Two for Guiding (different areas of the country, one at uni, one at home), one for rape crisis centre, one for music centre and one through Ofsted because I work as a part-time nanny. They're all dated within the last 2 years and they're all clear.'

> *Female, aged 18-24, West Midlands. Guider, teaches a Sunday school class, and helps out at a music centre with orchestral and choir rehearsals.*

These practical quibbles with the CRB process are not petty. As we argue below, the impact of the bureaucracy and cost of CRB-checking on volunteering has been considerable, and in its own way contributed to the formalisation of previously much more fluid voluntary engagements. However, what was most striking from our survey was the level of recognition that CRB checking could not possibly work as desired, as it could never anticipate what people might do the day after they had passed the CRB check:

> *There should be regular updates for the CRB as currently you can obtain a CRB, commit a crime next day and no one would know until another was applied for.*

>> *Female, 31-40, West Midlands. Not engaged in voluntary work.*

> *A CRB check only shows you haven't been caught yet!!!*

>> *Post on footy4kids discussion board, by a manager of an under-10s football team in Wolverhampton.*

Many respondents argued that CRB checks should take place more often, or that organisations should be able to access information immediately via a database. While there are logical reasons for this—it is true that

CRB checks only look for convictions in the past, which in theory frees people up to commit any number of offences once they have been 'cleared'—the proposal for a manner of 'continuous vetting' offered by some of our respondents is a disturbing one.

Once the principle of vetting is accepted it is difficult to establish limits to the power of surveillance. If adults require a security check before they are allowed near a child it follows that they need to be vetted on a regular basis. According to the logic that has led to the creation of the CRB, children must be protected not only from those who committed an offence in the past but also against those who may do so in the future. That is why it is inevitable that vetting is likely to become increasingly frequent and intrusive. The expansion of vetting will not make the system more efficient or effective since the institutionalisation of an expanding number of precautions cannot eliminate potential abusers of children.

Aside from its regrettable influence on inter-generational relations, the main accomplishment of the system of vetting is the undermining of civil liberties. It is a testimony to the powerful insecurities that surround intergenerational relations and child pro-tection that CRB checks have raised virtually no concerns about their implications for civil liberties. It is striking that, for all the objections raised by campaigners and the media to the proposed system of identity cards, and despite the widespread distrust of government, particularly when related to data collection and IT systems, the work of the Criminal

Records Bureau has raised very few objections. The centralisation of information about individuals, ranging from old offences to 'soft' information held by the police that did not result in formal action, represents a significant development in the routine surveillance of the whole population. The distribution of this information to potential employers or organisers of voluntary organisations (who are often, themselves, volunteers) represents a significant encroachment upon individuals' privacy, and their ability to control the information that other people have about them. We may accept that this is justified in relation to an individual attempting to hide a previous conviction for child sex offences. But the vast majority of those undergoing CRB checks have no such history, and the information collected and disseminated about these people can be both irrelevant (to their employment) yet damaging to their reputation.

The cost of CRB checks

In the early days of the Criminal Records Bureau, one of the principal concerns raised by the voluntary sector was the impact upon voluntary organisations of having to shoulder the cost of CRB checks. In 2008 this stood at £31 for a Standard Disclosure, and £36 for an Enhanced Disclosure—a substantial cost for any organisation working with children, particularly when using a large pool of volunteers. It was thus decided that CRB checks would be, in the words of the Criminal Record

Bureau's Fees and Service Standards, 'free of charge to volunteers'.[12]

However, it is important to understand that the national vetting scheme is not 'free of charge' to anybody. A bureaucracy that in 2008 employed 400 Home Office staff[13] and issued 300,000 Disclosures per month[14] is an expensive operation. Some of its costs will be met by business; but a significant proportion of those who are paid to work with children or vulnerable people—teachers, carers, healthcare workers—are employed by the public sector. The cost of CRB checks to public sector workers and volunteers is thus met by the taxpayer.

By January 2008, the Criminal Records Bureau (CRB) had issued its 15 millionth Disclosure.[15] The cost to business and society to that point can be estimated at around *half a billion pounds*—and that would be a gross underestimation. It assumes that the CRB processes only Standard Disclosures; it does not take into account the registration fee payable by organisations outside the voluntary sector; and it does not take into account the expenses and the proportion of the wages expended by chief executives and other highly paid and qualified individuals putting their staff through the CRB process.

The national vetting scheme also has a significant *time cost*. In 2008, the CRB was spending in the region of *92,000 working days* processing Disclosures. The time cost is of particular importance to voluntary organ-isations, for whom time is scarce, and non-remunerated. Those heading voluntary organisations have to spend an increasing amount of time on ensuring that their volunteers meet an expanding number of regulatory requirements, of which vetting is now an additional one. One chief executive of a national charity informed us: 'I wasted three and a half days of my busy life being police checked'. In 2008, we estimated that over the course of a single year, *at least 6 million days* are spent waiting for the result of CRB checks on volunteers. One can only speculate as to how this time might have been spent more positively and productively in the community. The ISA intends to streamline this process, but in a way that has considerable implications for civil liberties—and is unlikely in any case to reduce the overall time and cost burden of the national vetting scheme.

In terms of time and money, the national vetting scheme demands a considerable price from individuals, organisations and the public. But this is nothing compared to the cost it imposes on community life.

Putting people off

If CRB checks act as a barrier to undesirable adults becoming involved in voluntary work, that is all well and good. Since the tightening up of vetting procedures, however, there has been some concern that the hassle and sense of personal intrusion that accompanies a CRB check might 'put off' individuals who have a lot to offer. In a society that views volunteering as a social good, and where many organisations claim to have their activities hampered by a shortage of volunteers, this is a cause for concern.

The possibility that adults will be put off volunteering by the national vetting scheme is one of the 'unintended consequences' of an expanded vetting regime that 'places around nine million adults technically under suspicion of abuse'.[16] One volunteer manager of an under 13s cricket team told us of his frustration at losing his 'inspiring' coach who simply got 'fed up with the hassle and paperwork'. It is difficult to assess the extent to which prospective volunteers are deterred by CRB checks, as this falls into the category of 'proving a negative': one cannot know whether non-volunteers would have become involved if formal vetting procedures did not exist. However, anecdotal evidence suggests that there are a number of ways in which prospective volunteers are put off from making this contribution to community life.

- *Fear of being 'branded a paedophile'*

A survey published in June 2007 for children's charities NCH and Chance UK suggested that nearly one in five men do not volunteer to work with children because they would have to undertake a criminal records check.[17] The *Volunteer Survey 2007* further found that 13 per cent of men would not volunteer because they were worried people would think they were child abusers. In October 2007, a survey by Scotland's Commissioner for Children and Young People found that 48 per cent of adults said fear of being falsely accused of causing harm was a barrier to contact with children and young people, and that this would also make them less likely to help when they saw a young person in danger or distress.[18]

Commenting on the findings of the NCH/Chance UK survey, Hugh Thornberry, head of children's services at NCH, called for a better understanding of what CRB checks actually involved: 'Men need to know CRB checks are a painless process unless you have something to hide, and they are able to protect children.'

To a degree, it is possible to argue that some people's wariness about CRB checks is based on a misunderstanding of what they involve—while checking will reveal past offences, these offences only necessarily mean individuals will be prevented from volunteering if the offences pertain to children. However, it cannot be assumed that having a better understanding of the CRB process will be enough for individuals to risk putting themselves on the line. As well as the fear of rejection, individuals may understandably be reluctant to reveal sensitive information about their past—even if it is unlikely to bar them from working with children.

In an eloquent letter to the *Independent* newspaper in May 2007, a chair of governors at a primary school described the discomfort caused by CRB checking.[19] This school governor was informed by the local authority that a new appointee had a criminal record, and told of its details. 'The offence was minor, has no bearing on suitability to be in contact with children and was committed more than half a lifetime ago,' he wrote. But, in consequence:

I, as a volunteer, have information which I do not need to have, and if it became widely known in our small community, it could cause great distress. Now that CRB checks are necessary for almost all voluntary posts, information of this kind has the potential to be disseminated outside the control of the subject. The result is that this person will not volunteer to assist with any other community activities, and will carry this embarrassment for a lifetime.

The school governor concludes his letter by recognising that 'clearly children must be protected'. However, 'in this case and many others like it, no purpose has been served... The risk of disclosure of trivial indiscretions to those who have no need to know has the power to cause distress out of all proportion to the offence.'

• *A hassle and an imposition*

In the online survey we conducted for this research, the overwhelming problem raised with CRB checking was the hassle-factor, with several volunteers complaining about having to complete different CRB checks for every organisation they volunteered for. When asked if they knew anybody who had been put off volunteering by the CRB process, 28 per cent said that they did. For many of these, the reason was linked to a sense that their offers of help were being complicated and formalised by the vetting procedure:

> *They didn't feel that they should be screened as they were giving services voluntarily.*
>
> *Female Guider, 18-24, West Midlands.*

Not because of anything that they would hide - but the need to fill out forms, find suitable referees etc. Especially for a one-off type of volunteering such as making the refreshments at a week-long holiday club.

> *Female, aged 31-40, South East. Runs a church children's holiday club and teaches French at school on voluntary basis.*

By bureaucratising what were informal processes of 'helping out', vetting provides an implicit challenge to adults' sense that they should get involved. When the desire to help out leads first of all to an obstacle, in the shape of a form and a several-week delay before the volunteer can be presumed 'safe', this is the equivalent of presenting nascent volunteers with a sign asking, 'Are you sure about this?' The volunteers who pass the CRB test may then find themselves part of a small, struggling pool of 'safe' helpers, and roped in to do rather more than they wanted to. One mother of three young boys explains:

I often help out at the boys' football club—making tea, tying shoelaces and so on. Now they're very keen for me to have the CRB check done—and I really don't want it! Not because it will throw up any problems, but because I know once that's happened I'll be 'official'. I'll be expected to take on regular duties, and treated like I'm on some kind of committee. I never wanted that—I just wanted to help out here and there. But it looks like instead, I'll have to stay away and do nothing.

• *Trusting official technology*

The end of 2007 brought a series of scandals, where government departments managed to 'lose' sensitive data, to outcry from the press. The first and largest of these scandals was the Child Benefit debacle, in which two computer discs holding the personal details of all families in the UK with a child under 16 went missing. The data included the name, address, date of birth, National Insurance number and, where relevant, the bank details of 25 million people.[20]

Given the sensitivity of the kind of data revealed by CRB checks, it is surprising that there is not more concern about the potential for such large-scale data collection systems to go wrong, or for data to fall into the wrong hands. For the system can, and does, get things wrong. Home Office figures from 2006 showed that the CRB 'wrongly labelled 2,700 people as criminals: many consequently had a job offer withdrawn'.[21] An example of how badly wrong the checks can be was provided by a story in the Liverpool *Daily Echo* in January 2006: Robert Taylor, a grandfather, 'discovered he had a 33-year criminal record—even though he had never broken the law in his life. He was wrongly accused of being a rapist, a thug with a GBH conviction and a drink driver.'[22]

The shame and misery caused to individuals wrongly 'flagged' by CRB checks as posing a risk to children is considerable. They suffer not only the immediate, obvious penalty, of being barred from taking up their job or becoming involved in a voluntary organisation. They also bear the anxiety of other people knowing this information: information that, as the school governor quoted above put it in his letter to the *Independent*, 'if it became widely known... could cause great distress'. Given the understandable revulsion our society holds for convicted paedophiles, and the widespread belief that parents should be informed if there is a sex offender living in their midst, it is highly likely that the 'responsible person' in an organisation who receives the result of the CRB check may feel honour-bound to distribute that information more widely than he or she should. And what grounds would the victim of a CRB check that provided the wrong information have for rebutting that information in the immediate term, other than his or her word? In due course, after much official and legal wrangling, one would expect that the CRB would acknowledge its mistake, setting the applicant free to take up the position he or she originally applied for. But by then, the position would probably have been filled; and the stigma attached to the false allegation would remain ever-present.

It should also be noted that a system capable of getting it wrong about innocent people must also be capable of throwing up incorrect data about people who do pose a threat to children, thereby permitting their employment or involvement in voluntary organisations. It is of course true that a CRB check does not show what an individual has done, only whether he/she has been 'caught' doing it. This is of particular concern given that, by its very nature, the formal insistence on CRB checks privileges the data revealed by a technical process over the professional, or common sense, judgements made by the people involved in the institution or organisation. If a CRB check comes back as 'clear', some argue, this leads for a tendency for employers, colleagues and fellow volunteers to assume that everything is all right. As one female school governor in the North West explains:

> *The problem is that you end up with a tick-box approach to assessing people, rather than people making judgements on the basis of their experience. Personal and professional authority comes to count for less, and people stop looking out for real problems.*

There is a big difference between knowing somebody—their strengths, their weaknesses, and their personality—and, as one respondent to an online discussion on this issue put it, 'just see[ing] a bit of paper detailing an issue'. There is a danger that an over-reliance on technical systems will override the far more sensitive, balanced understanding that comes from knowing people. Reliance on technological solutions discourages grown-ups from using the insights they gained from experience to respond to the problems facing children. It distracts them from developing their intuition and understanding and may even encourage a flight from the making of professional judgments. What the system flags up outweighs what a carer's insight dictates.

Yet despite the real problems with technical systems for managing large amounts of sensitive data, and despite high levels of public mistrust about the competence of government and related authorities in managing these systems, there appears to be remarkably little public disquiet about the Criminal Records Bureau. In our survey, only one respondent cited the fact that people 'don't trust government systems' as a reason for people being put off from volunteering; while several respondents, frustrated by the slow and cumbersome character of the vetting process, seemed to be arguing for more institutions and organisations to have more access to more sensitive data more of the time. Such sentiments are testimony to the unrealistic expectations that many of us have about the efficacy and reliability of centralised databases.

Vetting and volunteering: An uneasy relationship

Our research has revealed a number of major concerns about the current national system of vetting. These concerns include:

- The shortcomings of the Criminal Records Bureau, widely reported in the UK press;

- The inconvenience and anxiety caused to prospective volunteers by having to undergo a CRB check;

- The widespread distrust of government's technical competence;

- The recognition that vetting has put off some people who should be volunteers and delayed the process of involvement for most volunteers;

- The recognition that ultimately CRB checks cannot prevent people from committing an offence after the check has taken place.

Yet, despite this raft of concerns, there seems to be a high level of acceptance of CRB checking amongst the public. To understand why this is, it is necessary to address the broader cultural and political context in which the national vetting scheme has been developed. This is one in which a heightened concern with protecting children from risk has thrown into question many of the activities, relationships and interactions that were once taken for granted as a normal, healthy part of community life.

Adults choose to help out with children's clubs and activities for a multitude of reasons. The common quality of volunteering, however, is a well-developed sense of adult responsibility. By definition, people who volunteer do not have to give up their time and energy: they choose to do it, for non-financial reward. By volunteering, people express the self-belief that they have something to offer the next generation, and the understanding that, as adults, they *should* offer themselves to do it. In this respect, volunteering to help with children's activities becomes one way in which adults feel that they are enriching their own lives and their communities at the same time.

Whether it was expressing a desire to teach children the right skills in football, to keep the power of 'pen, paper and creative thinking' alive, or to give Girl Guides today the same opportunities and experiences they themselves had as girls, respondents to our survey were keenly aware of the generational interplay within volunteering. Teaching the children skills and giving them access to experiences was balanced against an appreciation of what was in it for the adults: enjoyment, satisfaction, fun. This sentiment was best summed up by a man in his 60s, who had been a unit helper for Brownies and Guides for 32 years:

Passing on skills that the girls would not normally acquire. Being some one of the opposite sex they can talk to who isn't deemed a threat and is willing to listen to their problems. Being around young people keeps you feeling young even when you are getting long in the tooth. Feeling that you are giving something back to the community.

The sense of personal satisfaction that comes out of 'doing good' by younger generations embodies the most positive dynamic of relationships between generations. Adults are asserting the knowledge and responsibility they possess simply by being adults, for the sole reward of having a positive influence on the children under their supervision. It is this relationship that has operated, not simply through the voluntary sector but informally in the community, since the Enlightenment, allowing society to draw a clear distinction between adults and children and to rely on our collective ability to raise the next generation. That the same impulses are articulated through people engaged in community voluntary work today is to be welcomed.

The recent Labour government was keenly aware of the benefits of volunteering, promoting its importance in citizenship classes in schools and launching a 'Volunteers Week' in 2007 to encourage people to get involved. Yet, at the same time, it has also played a significant role in making life harder for voluntary organisations through the introduction of ever-tighter restrictions and regulations. As the Commission on the

Future of Volunteering warned in January 2008, 'too many people are being put off volunteering' by 'red tape and unnecessary bureaucracy'. The Commission claims that the government could best support volunteering by adopting a position of 'non-interference', arguing:

> It is time to rethink the obsession with any risks that might be involved and to remove financial obstacles which many people experience when they try to volunteer. We also need to avoid time-consuming criminal record checks, unless volunteers are working with children or vulnerable adults.[23]

We would go further, and argue that the dynamic of the national vetting scheme should be re-thought even in relation to voluntary organisations working with children. The implementation of a national vetting scheme directly challenges positive assumptions about the relationship between adults and children that until recently were taken for granted. The demand that adults be licensed before they can engage with children signals the sentiment that it should no longer be presumed that adults will have a positive, protective influence upon children. The very act of vetting makes the prior negative assumption that an adult's motivation for helping children could be malign, which further weakens the necessary bonds between generations in our communities.

Although proponents of the scheme contend that it is designed to prevent 'worst case scenarios', the very institutionalisation of the scheme encourages 'worst case scenario' assumptions to become the norm. One consequence of this process, we argue, is that adults feel increasingly nervous around children, unwilling and unable to exercise their authority and play a positive role in children's lives. Such intergenerational unease has not made children safer than in the past: if anything, it is creating the conditions for greater harm, as adults lose the nerve and will to look out for any child who is not their own. Perversely it inadvertently encourages grown-ups to avoid their responsibility for assuring the well-being of children in their community. This development is most striking amongst people in their late twenties and early thirties—many of whom have become estranged from the world of children and believe that they bear no responsibility for the well being of the younger generations.

2

Child Protection
and 'No Touch' Policies

The national vetting scheme is not the only measure that has been brought in over the past ten years to protect children from the possibility of abuse. As the Labour government's consultation document on the implementation of the Independent Safeguarding Authority pointed out, this is only one of ten such 'safeguarding' measures. The tightening-up of vetting procedures is, according to this document, inspired by the need to 'learn the lessons' of the Soham murders, and protect children from predatory strangers. Another important strand of the safeguarding legislation is, as the document claims, inspired by the need to 'learn the lessons' of the murder of Victoria Climbie: the eight-year-old who, in 2000, died at the hands of her aunt and aunt's partner following a horrific and sustained level of abuse.[1]

The policy framework that was brought about with reference to the official inquiry into Victoria Climbie's death is 'Every Child Matters'—a wide-ranging, far-reaching policy that provides for closer monitoring, regulating and information-sharing between institutions and organisations that deal with children. One of the policy outcomes fuelled by the Victoria Climbie inquiry was the creation of a £224 million centralised database, known as ContactPoint, on which schools, health authorities, social services, the police and other relevant authorities will store information about every child in the country, which can be accessed and 'shared' between these agencies.

The children's database has been criticised by a number of experts. Dr Eileen Munro of the LSE has organised two influential conferences drawing together some of the concerns about this database. As with the CRB system, one major concern is the reliance upon technical measures in place of professional judgement, which, critics argue, increase the possibility of information being wrongly inputted or interpreted; sensitive information falling into the wrong hands; and children's professionals suffering from 'information overload', thus finding themselves diverted from paying attention to the cases that most need it. The recent lost data scandals have caused a degree of official nervousness about this database, with the result that in November 2007 the government announced that it would be subject to an independent security check.[2] But despite all these serious reservations, the database — a project that seriously compromises the very essence of confidentiality—looks set to move full steam ahead.

The coexistence of the children's database, under the umbrella of Every Child Matters, with the national vetting scheme illustrates the extent to which regulation based on child protection has expanded over the past decade. Child protection policy does not limit itself to scrutinising *who* works with children, in order to weed out the minority of adults who might pose a threat; it increasingly legislates for *how* adults should interact with the children in their care. It selects who can be trusted as well as prescribing how that trust must be exercised. In recent years, child protection policy has become more stringent and centralised, so it has become increasingly proscriptive at the level of defining what is 'appropriate' contact, and what is not. This has led, some argue, to a situation where childcare professionals and other adults in positions of trust feel nervous and unsure about simply doing what is required to carry out their job.

In 2004-5, Heather Piper and colleagues at Manchester Metropolitan University conducted an ESRC-funded study into 'the problematics of touching between children and professionals'. Noting that 'the "touching" of children, as an aspect of professional practice [for example, the cuddling of young children] was causing concern', Piper's team investigated the way in which childcare professionals in the UK experienced the tension between children's need for nurturing contact and the fear that such contact may be interpreted as abuse. Reported injunctions included 'always having a second adult witness intimate care routines, minimising cuddling young children, even requiring particular ways of doing this, such as the sideways cuddle (to avoid any full-frontal contact)'.[3]

The research by Piper *et al* found that all respondents 'accepted that touch was essential to very young children and other young people'. Nonetheless:

Many respondents admitted feeling fearful of being regarded as physically or sexually abusive; behaved as though they did not trust themselves; had to prove to others (and vice versa) that they were innocent of any malevolent intent; did not trust others (adults and children) to judge their actions as innocent and appropriate; and did not trust children (and sometimes adults) to refrain from false or malicious allegations.

The dynamic behind this anxiety about touching was not motivated by the letter of child protection legislation: which does not, as Piper's team noted, formally limit physical contact between children and non-family carers. Rather, it was informed by the development of professional standards by bodies such as Ofsted and lack of certainty about how these standards might be interpreted during inspection processes, combined with a section of the National Care Standards that encourages staff to 'avoid putting themselves in a situation that may lead to allegations made against them'. In other words, the concern about touching children was not created by strict 'no touch' policies but by a more informally-filtered process of second-guessing, where professionals felt guarded in their interactions with children because of fears that others (children, colleagues, managers, inspectors) might misinterpret their actions. Professionals swiftly internalised caution about touching children, to the point where forms of defensive behaviour were experienced as a normal part of professional life. Piper explains:

When we started the research, some places would say they were touchy-feely places and didn't follow the rules. But we found very little difference between those, and the places that were following the rules.[4]

The internalisation of assumptions about child protection policy was also described by David Pearson, executive director of the Churches' Child Protection Advisory Service (CCPAS) and a former social worker. The problem, in Pearson's view, arises from a level of 'hysteria' about child protection, which means that people working with children think certain rules are enshrined in law or child protection policies when they are not. To that end, much of the recent work of the CCPAS has focused on trying to dispel some of the myths about what child protection rules should mean, and to develop 'good sense' child protection policies in their place. One of its recent leaflets deals with some commonly-experienced scenarios such as the assumption that two childcare workers need to accompany a child to the toilet; that childcare workers should not help a child apply sun-cream; that childcare workers should not hug a child who is upset. If better policies can be developed and promoted, in Pearson's view, this will help those working with children to feel supported while interacting with children in a way that best helps them—rather than covering one's back at the expense of a child's needs.

However, as the research by Heather Piper's team indicates, there is a limit to the extent to which more sensitive policy can counteract the problem of childcare workers feeling apprehension in their dealings with

33

children, and adopting 'odd behaviours' as a result. While the absence of clear guidelines spelling out exactly how adults are allowed to interact physically with children is often experienced by those working in such situations as a problem, attempts to formulate such guidelines inevitably prioritise a process of going by the book over the spontaneity and professional judgement that previously governed adult-child relations in professional settings. In their book on this subject,[5] Piper and Stronach call for 'a more ethical practice':

> ...one that encourages professionals not to slavishly follow 'no touch' guidelines, but to put touch back into context (i.e. relationships), and take account of trust and friendships. It is argued that we need to think through notions of 'free touch' just as much as we would 'free speech'. This is no call for license, but it is a call for recognition that any system that prioritises bureaucratic constraint over 'freedom' introduces a regime of unfreedoms that then develop—through a series of 'ratchet effects'—a kind of creeping totalitarianism, not to mention a galloping fatuity.

Impact on voluntary organisations

If the work of Piper's team illustrates the anxieties generated by child protection policies among those working with children in a professional capacity, we should consider how much more of a challenge is faced by those who interact with children through voluntary organisations. Volunteers will often not have the degree of training undergone by professionals; they will not have the same awareness of 'good practice'; and their fellow volunteers will often not be as well known to them as, say, teachers' trusted colleagues. Above all, voluntary organisations often bring together a diverse mix of individuals, brought together by their own volition and around their own interests, which can often make it difficult to know — let alone regulate — who might come through the door.

As David Pearson of CCPAS points out, this poses a distinct problem for faith organisations. While most organisations working with children are able to vet each adult who will come into contact with children, the church, by its very nature, 'holds its doors open to anyone'. It is known that church congregations do attract sex offenders, 'so inevitably people are coming in all the time who are in contact with children'. The challenge, says Pearson, is:

> [H]ow do we help the organisations we work with provide a safe service for children and meet the needs of children without distancing themselves from children in the way that many organisations have?[6]

For a faith group to slam its doors in the face of undesirable members would clearly undermine the purpose of its existence. Yet the church will remain particularly vulnerable to suspicions of abuse if it does not follow the prescribed practice. In a cultural climate that demands the licensing of adults before they can be presumed 'safe' with children, there is little opportunity for organisations to develop policies that are specific to their needs.

The expanding remit of child protection policies also poses a particular challenge in relation to sporting organisations. Dan Travis, a tennis coach based in Brighton and vocal critic of the national vetting scheme, argues:

> Vetting has had a massive impact. There are far fewer volunteers than there used to be. Most people I know think it is illegal to teach children without government permission in some form or another, be it local council or police.

For Travis, the effects of the national vetting scheme have been 'all negative'. 'It's very intrusive and leads to a climate of suspicion,' he argues. 'It does not make the children any safer and is a barrier to more activities happening.' Travis is also concerned about the 'secondary effects' brought about by the burgeoning child protection industry. 'The codes of conduct brought out by all sorts of governing bodies and quangos have paralysed many adults to the extent that they would rather do nothing than "the wrong thing"', he explains; while the kind of sport that is played has been changed to take into account an expanding list of concerns about safety and abuse.[7]

Sports coaching often necessarily involves physical contact with children, which can fall foul of 'no-touch' policies—either in the letter of the policies, or in individuals' interpretations of them. Furthermore, explains Travis, the definition of 'abuse' has widened so that, for example, age-old coaching practices can be defined as bullying, and thereby seen to contravene a sports club's child protection policy. Should sporting organisations disagree with this view, they are likely to find themselves without access to funding.

This situation is clarified by the work of the Child Protection in Sport Unit (CPSU). The CPSU was founded in 2001 as a partnership between the major child protection charity NSPCC and Sport England, the brand name of the English Sports Council, which is a distributor of Lottery funds to sport. In 2008, the CPSU website noted that 'each week more than eight million UK children take part in sport' in a range of situations, and that 'most enjoy themselves in safety'. However, 'a small number are at risk of abuse from individuals who choose sports work to gain access to children', and to this end the NSPCC 'works with the UK Sports Councils, governing bodies and other organisations to help them minimise the risk of child abuse during sporting activities'.[8]

The CPSU provides an example of a code of conduct recommended for sports organisations. Included in this code are the following instructions:

- Avoid contact or conduct that may be interpreted as having sexual connotations or which your sport defines as inappropriate

- Do not take part in or tolerate behaviour that frightens, embarrasses or demoralises an athlete or that negatively affects their self esteem

- Do not tolerate acts of aggression.[9]

The spirit of this code of conduct seems largely unobjectionable. Nobody wants their child, when taking part in a sporting activity, to be touched inappropriately, to be upset or humiliated, or to get into fights. Yet at the same time, we can surely recognise that one person's form of good coaching can be another's definition of bullying or demoralisation. We can also recognise that it is not always crystal clear what is, and is not, appropriate touching: indeed, rumours about 'pervy' PE teachers in schools have been circulated by children throughout the ages, by way of embarrassing unpopular physical education teachers who are simply doing their job. The passion historically associated with team sports has always had a tendency to lead to (often minor and easily-contained) 'acts of aggression'—in legislating against children expressing their commitment to their team, might this not take away much of the fun and excitement from their sport?

What looks like a common-sense child protection policy on paper is rarely so straightforward when applied to the messier reality of running a youth group, or coaching a football team. People have different standards and forms of behaviour; actions are open to misinterpretation; and there is a heightened awareness that falling foul of a child protection policy can have serious consequences for the individual. Is it any wonder that volunteers in this context choose to take the safest course of action, by remaining at arm's length—or not volunteering at all?

Formalising intergenerational encounters

The most regrettable outcome of child protection policies associated with vetting is the distancing of intergenerational relationships. Such policies foster a climate where adults feel uneasy about acting on their healthy intuition and feel forced to weigh up whether, and how, to interact with a child. Such calculated behaviour alters the quality of that interaction. It no longer represents an act that is founded on doing what a mentor feels is right—it is an act that is influenced by calculations about how it will be seen and interpreted by others and by anxieties that it should not be misinterpreted. In sport, the difference between a coach automatically reaching out to correct a child's position and a coach asking himself 'is this all right?' before doing so is that the former is a spontaneous action based on a desire to improve the child's game, and the latter is a timid gesture, reflecting an uncertainty about authority that the child must surely sense. In a community group, the difference between giving a distressed child a hug and asking that child 'would you like a hug?' is that the former is given as an unprompted expression of human compassion, and the latter is a transaction that requires a child's formal consent.

As previously noted, the majority of respondents to our survey considered themselves to be in favour of a national vetting system. When asked what they thought the impact of CRB checking had been upon the relationship between adults and children, many responded that it had had little impact, largely because the children were not aware of it. What emerged as more of a problem was the climate of suspicion towards the behaviour of adults in a child protection context. As one female school governor remarked, 'adults are more aware of child protection issues and are not putting themselves in situations that can be misconstrued'. The negative consequences of this tendency for adults to 'keep their distance' appeared to be felt particularly keenly among the Guiding community—including, interestingly, Guiders who are quite young themselves:

> It makes you a lot more wary about child protection. Just knowing that you have to be CRBd gets you thinking about how things might be misinterpreted such as physical contact. And sometimes that's detrimental to your relationship with the children, because you can't give an upset Rainbow a cuddle and they don't quite understand why. So the actual piece of paper makes no difference, but the CRB as a symbol of the culture we live in has a huge impact on the relationship.
>
> Female Guider, 18-24, West Midlands.

> I don't think CRBs have made any impact and don't think kids understand/know what they are. What does make an impact is all these regulations on 'child safety' if a seven-year-old is upset on pack hols, homesick etc. it's human nature to want to give them a hug and tell them its ok yet with these laws you don't seem to be able to comfort a child.
>
> Female Guider, 18-24, London.

> The general impression I have is that we are far more concerned about 'Safe From Harm' now (e.g. not being able to apply cream on a wound, give an upset child a hug etc in case it gives the wrong impression or we are accused of wrongdoing). A lot of the time we feel the need to protect ourselves as adults now, just in case. I don't feel CRBs have actually stopped this from happening, not only in the voluntary sector but also in the work sector. Though theoretically they should provide another form of protection.
>
> Female Guider, 25-30, West Midlands.

Without doubt, children need to be protected from those who may prey upon them. We would question, however, whether the policing and formalisation of intergenerational relations can contribute to the realisation of this objective. The policy of attempting to prevent paedophiles from getting in contact with children through a mass system of vetting may well unintentionally make the situation more complicated. One regrettable outcome of such policies is to estrange children from *all* adults—the very people who are likely to protect them from paedophiles and other dangers that they may face. The adult qualities of spontaneous compassion and commitment are, we argue, far more effective safeguarding methods than pieces of paper that promote the messages 'Keep Out' and 'Watch Your Back'.

The policy of vetting and the formalisation of inter-generational relations displaces the use of compassion, common sense and local knowledge with rules that appear perfectly sensible on paper but are often unhelpful in specific circumstances. During the course of our discussion it became evident that the application of formal procedures to the conduct of human relations threatens to deskill adults. Many adults often feel at a loss about how they should relate to youngsters who are not their children. When formal rules replace the exercise of compassion and initiative, adults become discouraged from developing the kind of skills that help them to relate, interact and socialise with children. We fear that this process of deskilling the exercise of adult authority may have the unfortunate consequence of diminishing the sense of responsibility that adults bear for the socialisation of the younger generation. Individuals who talked to us about the 'hassle of paperwork' also hinted that they were not sure that working with kids was 'worth the effort'. And if adults are not trusted to be near children, is it any surprise that at least some of them draw the conclusion that they are really not expected to take responsibility for the well-being of children in their community?

Experience indicates that the transition to adulthood is realised through gaining experience in dealing with the challenges of life. Through the internalisation of insights gained from such experience, adults learn to relate to the younger generations and in particular acquire confidence in exercising authority over them. The current obsession with rule-making undermines this crucial developmental process and indeed works towards deskilling adults who wish to exercise their authority.

3

'Health and Safety': Risk Aversion and the Fear of Litigation

Our survey asked respondents to indicate what they thought were the biggest problems facing voluntary organisations today, by ranking the following on a scale of one to five:

- Shortage of volunteers

- Shortage of children to take part in voluntary activities

- Parental worry

- Health and safety regulation

- Constraints on funding

Shortage of volunteers was identified as the biggest problem, followed by health and safety regulation. 'Parental worry' and 'shortage of children' were ranked last. As many of the explanatory responses indicated, 'health and safety regulation' is experienced as an independent dynamic to the fears that parents actually have for their children taking part in voluntary activities. The myriad rules and bureaucracies that now dominate voluntary work are often seen, not as a sensible precaution against actual harm, but an over-blown, politicised response to a culture of litigation and organisational self-protection:

The UK has now caught up with America in becoming a suing-based country. People are worried what they say, what they do and how they do it. Objectives are coming in from the likes of governing organisations that mean we might as well bubblewrap children.

Male junior football coach, aged 31-40, South East.

The shortage of volunteers is partly due to the problems of health and safety, and the culture of compensation. My husband was a scouter who left due to work, but says now that his work does not limit his time so much, he would not re-volunteer due to the fear of being sued by parents if a child got hurt, and due to the masses of paperwork required for every activity, e.g. qualifications, risk assessments, forms etc.

Female Guider, 25-30, West Midlands.

In recent years, there has been something of a backlash against the culture of risk-aversion surrounding children's activities. National newspapers regularly run stories decrying the stupidity of schools banning conker games in the playground; commentators are frequently heard discussing the problems caused to children by the decline in outdoor play; and the phrase 'Health and Safety' is often used as a pejorative shorthand for stupid rules that prevent people doing what they should, or want to, do.

In 2006, the first report of the government's Better Regulation Commission called for a more sensible approach to managing risk, including the recognition that risk can sometimes be beneficial; and the Health and Safety Executive launched a campaign against petty health and safety concerns, under the banner 'Get A Life'. In July 2007 Ed Balls, secretary of state for

Children, Schools and Families, made the headlines by pronouncing the virtues of conker games and the need for children to learn about risk through unsupervised play. Launching the government consultation *Staying Safe*, which aimed to 'strike the right balance between protecting their children whilst allowing them to learn and explore new situations safely', Balls argued:

> We want [our children] to be protected from harm and abuse. But this does not mean we should wrap them in cottonwool. Childhood is a time for learning and exploring.[1]

In January 2008, Prime Minister Gordon Brown set up a new watchdog, the Risk and Regulation Advisory Council, with the aim of developing 'a better approach to the understanding and management of public risk'.[2] This was widely hailed as an attempt by the government to untie some of the red tape: or, in the words of one news headline, 'Brown vows to fight nanny state culture that bans hanging baskets and conkers'.[3] Launching the Conservative Party's *Childhood Review* in February 2008, party leader David Cameron spoke of the 'duty' people have to discipline other people's children:

> Parents cannot and should not be with their children all of the time. We need adults to feel able to exert authority over and show compassion towards other people's children. This basic social responsibility, in many ways the mark of a civilised society, has been dramatically undermined by a risk-averse health and safety culture which, at times, has poisoned the relationship between adults and children.[4]

The recognition that risk-aversion can have a harmful impact upon the quality of childhood is a welcome, if overdue, development. It is what informs, for example, the work of the Campaign for Adventure, Risk and Enterprise in Society, which 'seeks to show that life is best approached in a spirit of exploration, adventure and enterprise' and calls for a better, more realistic appreciation of risk.[5] Ian Lewis, the campaign's co-ordinator and clerk for the All Party Parliamentary Group on Adventure and Risk in Society, argues that children today are facing 'the extinction of experience' through the focus on safety at the cost of adventure or excitement.[6]

Unfortunately, despite a growing awareness of the problems caused by risk avoidance, this still remains a central message in policy and culture: Ed Balls's *Staying Safe* consultation began with the admonition: 'Keeping children and young people safe is a top priority',[7] and when safety is flagged a top priority, the space allocated to healthy risk-taking is likely to be rather narrow and discrete. More importantly, the *idea* that children's safety is the top priority has become deeply culturally ingrained, with the result that adults automatically evaluate their children's activities with reference to the levels of risk involved. Children—and those in charge of them—cannot enjoy activities 'without a second thought' when the possibility of danger is ever-present, weighing like a conscience upon everything that children do.

Responding to our survey, one mother pinpointed the leap of faith that would be necessary to let children today participate in activities that 'previous generations of children enjoyed without a second thought'—even when, as a parent, one regrets their loss of freedom:

> [The problem is] not allowing children to grow up with the freedom that we had when we were kids. My sister and brother and myself would go out on our bikes in the morning and come back when we were hungry. Mum did worry about us but knew that we were safe and yet I will not let my kids go to the park on their own even though I can see them from our bedroom window!

The apparent backlash against 'health and safety gone mad' contains some spirited insights, and there have been thoughtful suggestions from some quarters about how policymakers might go about supporting a culture of healthy risk-taking. Ultimately, however, this backlash is unlikely to alter the premise of existing policy. Why? Because as long as intergenerational relations are perceived as a high-risk experience children will continue to be discouraged from pursuing independent activities freely in the outdoors. Sadly none of the recent calls to challenge the dominance of risk-aversion over childhood have attempted to address the principal force that is driving it: the intense sense of mistrust towards adult motives, particularly those of strangers. As long as adults are perceived as potential threats to children it is difficult for parents not to feel permanently anxious about their youngsters' safety.

Responsibility aversion

Alongside the growing policy concern about the impact of excessive risk-aversion on childhood experience, there is now an increasing realisation that an obsessive focus on risk and procedure can actually make society more dangerous. When adults become paralysed by the injunction to follow the rules at the expense of their instincts, tragic consequences may follow. Two high-profile news stories from 2007 grimly illustrate this problem. In January 2007 Paul Waugh, a coastguard in Cleveland, climbed down a cliff in high winds to rescue a stranded 13-year-old girl, without waiting to fit safety harnesses upon himself. He was criticised by the Maritime and Coastguard Agency for failing to meet health and safety procedures, and has resigned in disgust.[8] In May 2007 Jordon Lyon, a 10-year-old boy, died after jumping into a pond to rescue his step-sister from drowning. Two police community support officers failed to help because they lacked training in 'water rescue': a decision supported as 'proper' by Greater Manchester Police.[9]

Cases such as these provoke widespread media and public disquiet. It is heartening to note that Paul Waugh was hailed as a hero by everyone but the Maritime and Coastguard Agency and that most people would jump into a pond to save a little boy. And many would have sympathy with Sir Norman Bettison, chief constable of West Yorkshire Police, who, in recalling the incident in Oxfordshire in 2004 when two women were shot at a barbecue party and died because police and ambulance crews had been ordered to stay at a safe distance, accused the 'health and safety Taliban' of stopping police from serving the public. 'I can tell you, as a police professional with some experience of firearms incidents, that it is the health and safety zealots who are responsible', he said. [10] But can health and safety 'zealots' really be held responsible for the extent to which risk aversion has been taken on board by people—professionals, volunteers, and citizens—across the board?

Many adults will, at some time in their lives, have wondered whether they possess the mettle to save somebody from a burning building or to dive in front of a gun-man embarking on a school massacre. There is a hope that, in these circumstances, the instinct to protect will overcome the rational understanding that acting upon this instinct is likely to mean death or significant injury: that not thinking twice about acting will enable the individual to act. Thankfully, most of us are never put to the test in these circumstances. On a daily basis, however, adults are confronted with mundane, everyday scenarios that involve no risk to life or limb—but which these days throw people into a state of moral confusion.

The story everyone remembers is the one about a two-year-old girl who disappeared from her nursery and drowned in a garden pond. A bricklayer had driven past her as she wandered through the village. 'She wasn't walking in a straight line. She was tottering. I kept thinking, "Should I go back?"' he told the inquest into the child's death. 'One reason I did not go back is because I thought someone would see me and think I was trying to abduct her.' [11] In our research for this report, many people remembered this story yet could not remember the details—when it happened, where it happened—but they remembered it because something similar (though less drastic) had happened to them, or a friend of theirs. This disturbing story, of a child disappearing because the adult who saw her thought twice and chose to cover his back rather than help her out, has attained the status of an urban myth, and is used as the backdrop to discussions about whether you might help a child climb down from a climbing frame, whether you would intervene in a nasty fight between children, whether you would help a child find her way home, whether you would pick up and cuddle a toddler who had fallen over, whether you would administer basic First Aid on a child you did not know in a public playground if you did not hold a certificate…

People worry about these things because of the sense that, still, 'everyone knows' that it is right to help and comfort a lost, hurt, or frightened child—but at the same time, 'in this day and age', to do so is foolhardy. Thus, a human response that was once spontaneous has been interrupted by warning bells, making people think twice about something that, in the recent past, they would simply have done. The health and safety concerns that are used as justification for inaction, for example in the drowning of Jordon Lyon, are not necessarily reasons why people do not act in the way they know to be right. Rather, they are post-hoc rationalisations, which enter into the hesitation between spontaneous action and the decision to cover one's back. Controlling the excesses of 'health and safety zealots' is something that clearly needs to be done—but we should recognise that the problem is not the existence of 'silly rules' so much as the crisis of adult confidence that encourages people to take these rules on board.

The principal outcome of these trends for intergenerational relations is not simply an aversion to risk but to responsibility. Adults who used to absorb some of the risks faced by children are often not inclined to continue to do so, in case their behaviour is misinterpreted. Is it any surprise that there is now a generation of adults who have acquired the habit of distancing themselves from children and young people? From their perspective, intergenerational relations are experienced as an inconvenience from which they would rather be exempt. Even professionals who work with children are under pressure to avoid taking responsibility. Their career depends more on ticking the right boxes than exercising professional judgement.

4

Disconnection and Distrust

As traditional communities have become fragmented and confused, traditional 'ways of doing things' have been thrown into question, whether that be hugging an upset child or telling off an unruly teenager. There is a palpable sense that the rules have changed from when we were children—we can no longer act in the way that we think is right, learned from our parents and our childhood; instead we feel bound to act in a way that others would deem 'appropriate', in case our actions and motivations are misconstrued. This gives rise to a high level of intergenerational tension, where adults feel estranged from each other and from their children, and tentatively try to navigate relationships according to rules and conventions that are far from clear.

In a 1997 study carried out for the University of Kent, Frank Furedi and Tracey Brown sought to understand the tension between the elderly and younger generations. The study found that elderly people, often having little direct contact with children and unsure as to what the 'new rules' were, felt extremely isolated and unsure of themselves. They felt they had little to offer the younger generation, and that anything they might have to offer may be deemed wrong. An 82-year-old man with several grandchildren provided an example of how new conventions regarding the relationships between adults and children create confusion for the elderly:

> I'll give you an instance of what happened to me last week. I was in a shop and this woman came in who the wife knew, with her little granddaughter. I was eating a sweet and this little girl looked at me, so I said, 'would you like a sweetie, duck?' She got all scared and jumped back. And I said, 'well that's the best thing you want to do. Never take sweeties off nobody.' She done right, but it made me feel cheap, like. It made me feel awful really, to think I was offering a little girl a sweet... and I love kiddies. In the paper you hear there's horrible people about and it's awful, but it made me feel right cheap.[1]

Our current research has indicated that this process of distrust and self-doubt has spread rapidly in the intervening years, across age groups and to other forms of interaction between adults and children. Adults today would probably not dream of offering sweets to strange children—they even think twice about comforting a distressed toddler, or helping a child in trouble, in case their actions are misconstrued. And this anxiety about spontaneous action is not confined to the elderly, but evident among people actively engaged in children's activities; even parents themselves.

We have noted how, for example, even young Guide leaders (aged 18-24) were confused and defensive about how they should interact with children in their care—their own experience and upbringing told them that they should 'give an upset Rainbow a cuddle', but they were keenly aware of the rules that barred them from doing so. We have also noted how parents, who need to be CRB checked before becoming engaged in voluntary activities with other people's children, are beginning to feel the need to proclaim their CRB status in informal settings, such as their own homes. Even when it comes to their own children, parents are increasingly concerned about the misinterpretation of their actions by other adults. One thread on the 'Dad's Lifestyle' discussion boards of the Netmums website[2] is posted by 'Karina M' on behalf of her partner:

> He's taking our two-year-old son out swimming at the moment and called me whilst waiting for the pool to open. It seems that the mothers in the cafe he was waiting in were giving him filthy looks (apparently when he walked in it was like a scene from a Western when the room goes silent and tumbleweed blows across the foreground). This happens whenever he goes out with our son on his own, especially if he takes him into a joint changing/feeding room. Now, there is nothing strange looking about him, he's a perfectly normal guy, so I was just wondering if any other dads out there have the same experience? He's considering stapling his police check to his forehead every time he goes out! Any feedback or opinions would be greatly appreciated.

Karina M received many responses from mothers and fathers providing their own similar experiences. These included 'Helen G', who described how her husband had taken their four-year-old ice-skating and was holding her hand: 'A marshall came up to him and actually asked him if he was her dad.' 'Jim T', a stay-at-home dad, wrote:

> It's the biggest bugbear of the job. In fact the swimming scenario is the worst, 'cause it can actually make you feel like you must be a

pervert. When I'ckle Bob was six months we went to water babies and the reception was damn right disgraceful... Eventually it does get better, once they get to know you, and realise that you are just doing the same as them and not just there to cop off and perv at folk.

Returning to the discussion thread, 'Karina M' thoughtfully wondered, '[I]f other women are reacting like this, are we guilty of doing it ourselves without realising? I'm sure if you asked the people that we've seen doing it, they'd answer no...'

This exchange hints at the degree to which distrust of other adults has become internalised. Adults' innate sense of responsibility for children, which used to be expressed in comforting, helping or watching out for other children, has been replaced by an automatic hostility to adults seen with children who are presumed to be not their own. We should question whether there is anything healthy, or helpful, in a response where communities look at children's own fathers with suspicion, but would balk at helping a lost child find their way home.

5

Conclusion and Recommendations

The crisis of intergenerational trust is a complex cultural problem. It would be one-sided to argue that policy developments such as the national vetting and barring scheme have created this problem, and that removing them would solve things overnight. However, our research suggests that the creation of a probationary licence for adults through the national vetting scheme exacerbates the breakdown of trust within communities and throws assumptions about adult authority and responsibility into question in a way that mitigates against people stepping in to help children out when things go wrong.

We would argue that, at a policy level, what is needed is both *enlightened policy*, which puts greater trust in the ability of professionals and volunteers to act on their instincts and less pressure upon them to cover their backs; and *less policy*: putting a halt to the juggernaut of regulation and behaviour codes that make voluntary organisations increasingly difficult to run, and volunteers resentful and unsure of themselves. As the government evaluates the national vetting scheme, we suggest that it pays at least as much attention to the consequences in terms of deterring 'good' volunteers as it does to the scheme's effectiveness in keeping 'bad' volunteers out. Greater scrutiny should be applied to the work of what has been termed 'the child protection industry', and the often unforeseen, but nonetheless negative, consequences of the regulations, systems and policies that are put into place in the name of 'safeguarding'.

There is also the need for *sustained public discussion* of the issues raised in this report. The thoughtful responses given to our online survey suggest that people are highly aware that the relationship between adults and children today has become fraught, and they are attempting to find ways to resolve this that make sense to them. If we believe that adult society, as a whole, wants to help children rather than harm them, we should move the discussion beyond its contemporary fixation with 'predatory paedophiles' to address wider, and frankly more pressing, concerns.

However the single most important problem that needs to be addressed is how society can affirm and support the exercise of adult authority through acts of solidarity and collaboration. The growing distancing of generational encounters can only be fixed through providing adults with greater opportunity to interact with children. Adults need to be encouraged to exercise their responsibility towards the guiding and socialising of young people. That means that we need to question and challenge cultural assumptions that automatically throw suspicion on the exercise of adult authority.

It is time that we had a national review of all the procedures that regulate generational relations and drew up a balance sheet of their impact on community life. We believe that such a review would conclusively show the need for substantial deregulation of generational relationships. A national review would not only improve and clarify the exercise of adult authority: it would carry the potential for changing cultural attitudes to the way that grown-ups are perceived.

Notes

Introduction to the Second Edition

1 The Safeguarding Vulnerable Groups Act 2006.
http://www.opsi.gov.uk/acts/acts2006/ukpga_20060047_en_1

2 'Q&A: Vetting and barring scheme'. BBC News Online, 11
September 2009;
http://news.bbc.co.uk/1/hi/education/8156124.stm
Sir Roger's review was published in December 2009 as
'Drawing the Line' - A report on the Government's Vetting and
Barring Scheme;
http://publications.everychildmatters.gov.uk/eOrderingDow
nload/DCSF-01122-2009.pdf

3 Government accepts all Sir Roger Singleton's
recommendations on vetting and barring. DCSF Press
Release, 14 December 2009;
http://www.dcsf.gov.uk/pns/DisplayPN.cgi?pn_id=2009_024
7

4 'Parent drivers "shouldn't over-react to vetting moves"',
Daily Telegraph, 14 September 2009;
http://www.telegraph.co.uk/news/uknews/6184668/Pa
rent-drivers-shouldnt-over-react-to-vetting-
moves.html

5 'Vetting and barring facts'. DCSF, 8 February 2010. Accessed
30 March 2010;
http://www.dcsf.gov.uk/news/index.cfm?event=news.i
tem&id=vetting_and_barring_myth_buster

6 'Parents who ferry children to clubs face criminal record
checks', Guardian, 11 September 2009;
http://www.guardian.co.uk/uk/2009/sep/11/criminal-
checks-parents-scouts

7 'Now parents face criminal checks just to enter their
children's school,' Daily Mail, 7 December 2009; 'Now even

Sunday-school parents must be vetted,' *Sunday Telegraph*, 1 November 2009; 'Schools vet parents for Christmas festivities,' *Sunday Times*, 29 November 2009.

8 'Vetting and barring facts', DCSF, 8 February 2010. Accessed 30 March 2010; http://www.dcsf.gov.uk/news/index.cfm?event=news.item&id=vetting_and_barring_myth_buster

9 'Now parents face criminal checks just to enter their children's school', *Daily Mail*, 7 December 2009; http://www.dailymail.co.uk/news/article-1233822/School-bans-visitors-criminal-checks-extreme-crack-down.html

10 'Council bans parents from play areas', *Daily Telegraph*, 28 October 2009; http://www.telegraph.co.uk/news/newstopics/politics/lawandorder/6453268/Council-bans-parents-from-play-areas.html

11 'Children's care crisis as criminal vetting fees approach £600m', *Observer*, 23 August 2009; http://www.guardian.co.uk/society/2009/aug/23/criminal-record-bureau-checks-children

12 'Eleven million names on school vetting database', *Independent*, 17 July 2009; http://www.independent.co.uk/news/education/education-news/eleven-million-names-on-school-vetting-database-1750103.html

'Nine million face paedophile checks despite Ed Balls U-turn', *Daily Telegraph*, 14 December 2009; http://www.independent.co.uk/news/education/education-news/eleven-million-names-on-school-vetting-database-1750103.html

13 'Child safety vetting list will grow from initial 9m', BBC News Online, 14 December 2009; http://news.bbc.co.uk/1/hi/education/8412450.stm

14 'Criminal record checks gone too far', *Daily Telegraph*, 30 October 2009; http://www.telegraph.co.uk/news/newstopics/politics/lawandorder/6461335/Criminal-record-checks-gone-too-far.html

15 'Big Brother database on adults working with children may ruin innocent lives, warns watchdog', *Daily Mail*, 11 June 2009; http://www.dailymail.co.uk/news/article-1192207/Big-Brother-database-adults-working-children-ruin-innocent-lives-warns-watchdog.html

16 'Vetting blunders label 12,000 innocent people as paedophiles, violent thugs and thieves,' *Daily Mail*, 13 November 2008; 'Innocent victims of CRB blunders receive just £223 compensation,' *Daily Telegraph*, 26 January 2009.

17 'Q&A: Vetting and barring scheme'. BBC News Online, 11 September 2009; http://news.bbc.co.uk/1/hi/education/8156124.stm The Vetting and Barring Scheme Guidance, HM Government, March 2010; http://www.isa-gov.org.uk/PDF/VBS_guidance_ed1_2010.pdf

Preface to the First Edition

1 Furedi, F., *Paranoid Parenting: Abandon Your Anxieties and be a Good Parent*, London: Allen Lane (The Penguin Press), 2001.

1: CRB Checks: Barriers to Involvement

1 Department for Children, Schools and Families; Home Office; Department of Health, *SVG Act 2006: ISA scheme Consultation Document*, 14 November 2007:

http://www.dfes.gov.uk/consultations/downloadableDocs/S
VG%20Act%20ISA%20consultation%20final.pdf

2   *The Case Against Vetting: How the child protection industry is
    poisoning adult-child relations*, Manifesto Club, 16 October
    2006:
    http://www.manifestoclub.com/files/THE%20CASE%20AGA
    INST%20VETTING.pdf

3   'Children's cost in safety bill', Letter to *The Times* (London),
    16 October 2006:
    http://www.timesonline.co.uk/article/0,,59-2405362,00.html

4   Campaign Against Vetting Briefing Document. Manifesto
    Club, April 2008:
    http://www.manifestoclub.com/files/ISA%20Briefing%20Doc
    ument.pdf
    Reported in *The Times* (London), 10 April 2008: 'Vetting for
    restaurants and shops that hire children to work weekends':
    http://www.timesonline.co.uk/tol/news/uk/article3716359.ec
    e

5   'Parents get new sex crime checks', *BBC News*, 17 February
    2008: http://news.bbc.co.uk:80/1/hi/uk/7249043.stm

6   'Chaos in schools on first day back', *BBC News*, 4 September
    2002: http://news.bbc.co.uk/1/hi/education/2236912.stm

7   'History of checks U-turns', *BBC News*, 4 September 2002:
    http://news.bbc.co.uk/1/hi/education/2237173.stm

8   'Errors over teacher criminal checks', *BBC News*, 12 April
    2007: http://news.bbc.co.uk/1/hi/england/6529947.stm

9   DCSF; Home Office; Department of Health, *SVG Act 2006:
    ISA scheme Consultation Document*. 14 November 2007, p. 1.

10 DCSF; Home Office; Department of Health, *SVG Act 2006:
    ISA scheme Consultation Document*. 14 November 2007, p. 1.

11 Interview with Jennie Bristow, 8 January 2008.

12 *DIP 009 - Fees and Service Standards,* Criminal Records Bureau
    website. Accessed 14 February 2008:
    http://www.crb.gov.uk/default.aspx?page=1863

13 *CRB Annual Report and Accounts 2006-07:*
    http://www.crb.gov.uk/pdf/Annual%20Report%20&%20Acc
    ounts%202006-07.pdf

14 CRB. *Disclosure News - Issue 58,* January 2008:
    http://www.crb.gov.uk/default.aspx?page=4936

15 CRB. *Disclosure News - Issue 58,* January 2008.
    http://www.crb.gov.uk/default.aspx?page=4936

16 Gill, T., *No Fear: Growing up in a risk averse society,* London:
    Calouste Gulbenkian Foundation, 2007, p. 46.

17 'Paedophile stigma puts off men from volunteering', *The
    Express,* 2 June 2007.

18 'Adults "too afraid" of youth work', *BBC News,* 16 October
    2007: http://news.bbc.co.uk/1/hi/scotland/7045544.stm

19 'A trivial arrest, but a lasting distress', Letters to the Editor,
    The Independent (London), 23 May 2007.

20 'UK's families put on fraud alert', *BBC News,* 20 November
    2007:
    http://news.bbc.co.uk/1/hi/uk_politics/7103566.stm

21 Gill, *No Fear: Growing up in a risk averse society,* 2007, p. 48.

22 'CRB vows to learn from its mistakes', *Liverpool Daily Echo,*
    20 June 2007.

23 Commission on the Future of Volunteering. 'Press release:
    Willing and able volunteers stifled by red tape and
    bureaucratic hurdles', 28 January 2008:
    http://www.volcomm.org.uk/news/Willing+and+able+volunt
    eers+stifled+by+red+tape+and+bureaucratic+hurdles.htm

Report of the Commission on the Future of Volunteering and Manifesto for Change, 28 January 2008:
http://www.volcomm.org.uk/NR/rdonlyres/0B8EC40C-C9C5-454B-B212-C8918EF543F0/0/Manifesto_final.pdf

2: Child Protection and 'No Touch' Policies

1   Department for Children, Schools and Families; Home Office; Department of Health, *SVG Act 2006: ISA scheme Consultation Document,* 14 November 2007:
http://www.dfes.gov.uk/consultations/downloadableDocs/SVG%20Act%20ISA%20consultation%20final.pdf

2   Doward, J. and Kelbie, P.,'Fresh fears over child benefit as more records go missing', *Observer,* 25 November 2007:
http://www.guardian.co.uk/politics/2007/nov/25/immigrationpolicy.economy

3   Piper, H. *et al.*, 'Touchlines: The problematics of touching between children and professionals', ESRC-funded research project RES-000-22-0815.

4   Interview with Jennie Bristow, 17 December 2007.

5   Piper, H. and Stronach, I., *Don't Touch! The educational story of a panic,* London: Routledge, 2008.

6   Interview with Jennie Bristow, 24 January 2008.

7   Interview with Jennie Bristow, 15 January 2008.

8   CPSU homepage. Accessed 13 February 2008:
http://www.thecpsu.org.uk/Scripts/content/Default.asp

9   'Child Protection in Practice', CPSU website. Accessed 13 February 2008:
http://www.thecpsu.org.uk/Scripts/content/Default.asp?Page=OrgsChildProtection&MenuPos=Left&Menu=2344&Sel=0400

3: Health and Safety: Risk Aversion and the Fear of Litigation

1   Frean, A., 'Bring back the conker fight to re-educate cottonwool kids', *The Times* (London), 18 July 2007: http://www.timesonline.co.uk/tol/news/uk/education/article 2094007.ece

2   Department for Business, Enterprise and Regulatory Reform press release, 'PM calls for a better approach to the understanding and management of public risk', 16 January 2008.

3   Doughty, S., 'Brown vows to fight nanny state culture that bans hanging baskets and conkers', *Daily Mail*, 16 January 2008: http://www.dailymail.co.uk/pages/live/articles/news/ news.html?in_article_id=508635&in_page_id=1770

4   Elliott, F. and Frean, A., 'Telling off other people's children is everyone's duty, says Cameron', *The Times* (London), 5 February 2008: http://www.timesonline.co.uk/tol/news/politics/article330862 9.ece

5   Campaign for Adventure, Risk and Enterprise in Society website. Accessed 13 February 2008: http://www.campaignforadventure.org/

6   Interview with Jennie Bristow, 20 December 2007.

7   Department for Children, Schools and Families, *Staying safe: a consultation document, Summary*, 2007: http://www.dfes.gov.uk/consultations/downloadableDocs/71 61-StayingSafeSUMMARY.pdf

8   'Coastguard who saved girl twice quits over health and safety row', *The Times* (London), 12 January 2008: http://www.timesonline.co.uk/tol/news/uk/article3174645.ec e

9   Kennedy, D., 'Failure to save dying boy prompts call to scrap "community" police', *The Times* (London), 22 September 2007: http://www.timesonline.co.uk/tol/news/uk/article2505301.ece

10 'Gordon Brown takes on the health and safety zealots', *Sunday Times* (London), 20 January 2008.

11 'Mum's agony as she finds tot, 2, under water', *Daily Mirror*, 22 March 2006.

4: Disconnection and Distrust

1   Furedi, F. and Brown, T., *Disconnected: Ageing in an alien world*, University of Kent, 1997.

2   Netmums Coffeehouse: Lifestyle Boards. Accessed 13 February 2008: http://www.netmums.com/coffeehouse/lifestyle-8/dads-lifestyle-255/63110-hes-not-pervert.html